BIG TIMES IN A SMALL TOWN

CHRISTINE LAVIN PRESENTS
THE VINEYARD TAPES

HIGHLIGHTS OF THE FIRST ANNUAL MARTHA'S
VINEYARD SINGER/SONGWRITERS' RETREAT:
LIVE AT THE WINTERTIDE COFFEEHOUSE

Edited by Milton Okun

The First Annual
Martha's Vineyard
Singer/Songwriters' Retreat

Starting the day after Labor Day until the end of September, I invited singer/songwriters from all over the U.S. to get together, talk shop and make music. Over the month the group included Richard Shindell, Buddy Mondlock, Hugh Blumenfeld, Andrea Gains, Cheryl Wheeler, Anne Hills, Patty Larkin, John Forster, David Wilcox, Nance Pettit, David Roth, Andrew Ratshin, Hilary Field, Sally Fingerett, Dan Green, David Buskin, James Mee, Megon McDonough, Julie Gold, Howard Morgen, Estelle Morgen, Elizabeth Bunker, Pierce Pettis, Raymond Gonzalez and Amy Malkoff, Grant King, Susie Burke, David Surette, Mike Connelly, Peter Primont, Sheila Primont, Kevin Sheehan, Cliff Eberhardt, Scott Alarik, Peter Nelson, Diane Nelson, Kristina Olsen, Barbara Kessler, David Massengill, Ellen Cross, Kathy Moran, Pam Lewis, Vic & Reba Heyman, Geoff Bartley, Kate Taylor, Charlie Witham, Chris Smither, Jim Infantino, Lloyd Donnelly, Frank Coakley, Red Grammer, Leslie Nuchow, Suzi Katz, David Seitz, Greg Greenway, Chuck Pyle, Nancy Moran, and Fett.

We had a great time being together, and thanks to the efforts of Tony Lombardi and his staff of volunteers, we were also able to perform 11 concerts at The Wintertide Coffeehouse in Vineyard Haven. David Seitz, both a doctor and a recording engineer, drove up from New York City every weekend to tape our shows, which totaled over 30 hours of music. It was difficult deciding which cuts to include—there were *so many* great songs performed during the month. This is just a sampling of what went on.

Christine Lavin

Chris Lavin, Jonatha Brooke, Patty Larkin, Sally Fingerett: "The Girls' Lipstick Club"

Contents

Piano/Vocal Arrangements: Edwin McLean, Mark Phillips,
and Jon Chappell
Music Engraving: Edwin McLean, Mark Phillips,
and Jon Chappell
Production Manager: Daniel Rosenbaum
Creative Manager: Len Handler
Art Direction: Rosemary Jenkins
Director Of Music: Mark Phillips

All photos by Betsy Corsiglia originally appeared in The Martha's
Vineyard Times. *Used by permission of* The Martha's Vineyard Times

All photos by Alison Shaw originally appeared in the Vineyard Gazette.
Used by permission of Alison Shaw.

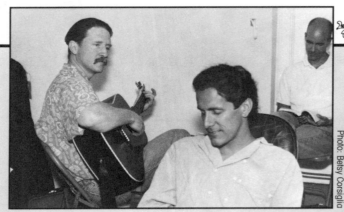

James Mee, David Roth and Grant King

Photo: Betsy Corsiglia

David Wilcox and Andrew Ratshin onstage at the Wintertide

Photo: Betsy Corsiglia

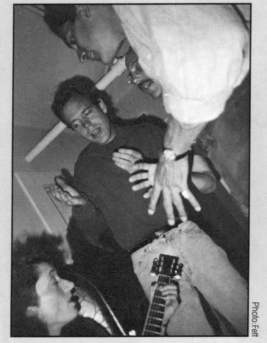

Patty Larkin & the "Daves",
Wilcox, Buskin, Roth

Photo: Felt

David Buskin

Photo: Alison Shaw

Kristina Olsen and her sweetie, Michael Ernst

Photo: Betsy Corsiglia

The Wintertide

Nancy Moran & Tony Lombardi

Photo: Felt

Guitar instructor Howard Morgen and David Buskin

Photo: Betsy Corsiglia

Hilary Field & Andrew Ratshin

Photo: Nancy Moran

Howard & Estelle Morgan

Photo: Nancy Moran

Christine Lavin & Rayeanne King

Photo: Alison Show

The Wintertide

Big Times In A Small Town

Words and Music by
James Mee

9

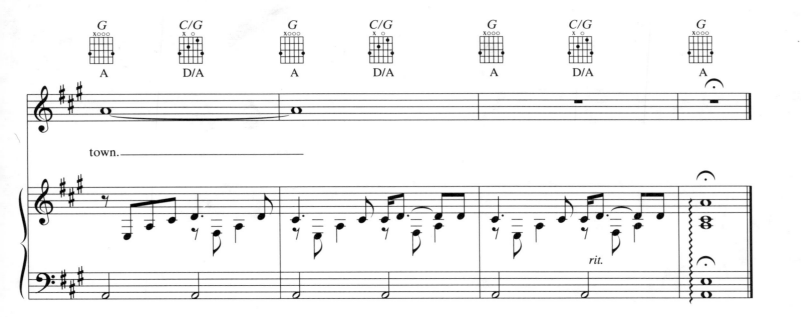

town._____

rit.

Additional Lyrics

3. You see the girls grow up and they make new homes.
   They marry boys they've always known.
   High school sweethearts, hearts on a tree.
   The river moves on quietly.

4. Boys on the back roads drinking wine,
   Dreaming the dreams their fathers left behind.
   Sometimes I'd wonder what the future would bring.
   And the river whispered, "Hey boy, nothin' but the same
       old things." *(To Chorus)*

5. Well, I'm eating French fries all covered in gravy.
   I'm talking with the Saint Ann Hall bingo ladies.
   And suddenly I remember as I'm walking down these streets,
   This town runs through my veins and that river
       runs deep.*(To Chorus)*

Dog Dreams

Words and Music by
Jonatha Brooke Mallet

We're gon - na run o - ver all_____ the neigh - bor - hood_____

cats,   'cause they

tease   us_____ from_____   the oth - er_____   side   of_____ the

fence._____

Tacet

Please don't— wake us— up.—

No

Chorus

bad dog, no stay, no base-ment, no way,— no—

choke chain, no dry food, no fetch game, no, no, no. No

sit, lie down, roll o - ver, shame.____

*bad dog, no stay, no base- ment, no way,____ no____

*2nd and 3rd times lead vocal ad lib

choke chain, no dry food, no fetch game, no, no, no. No

17

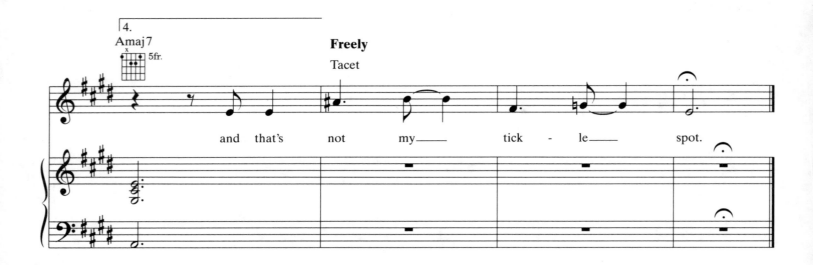

Additional Lyrics

2. Me and Rex took the car,
Ha ha, stay home ... stay.
We're gonna go through everyone's garbage
Have the dinners we deserve.
We're gonna find some
Great-smelling bitches
And see if they meant what they said
From the end of the leash.

Dog dreams, dog dreams.
Please don't hose us off! (*To Chorus*)

Summer Of Love

Words and Music by
Peter N. Nelson

Moderately slow, in 2

1. When I was fif - teen and a man of the world,——— I was

mf

2.3. *See additional lyrics*

3rd time, repeat 1st 32 bars of Verse.

mad - ly in love with a Cath - 'lic girl. She had gray I - rish eyes and the

whit - est of teeth, and a bod - y that left the whole neigh - bor - hood weak. It was a

bod - y a ful - ly grown wom - an should have, in the spring of her years, in the

some oth-er guy.— 1.2. And I'd sing: Shawn, where have you gone?— It's nine -

3. *Instrumental*

teen - six-ty-eight— and the Bea-tles are on.— I've got

nine cig-a-rettes, that should last— us till dawn.

Oh— Shawn,— where have you

22

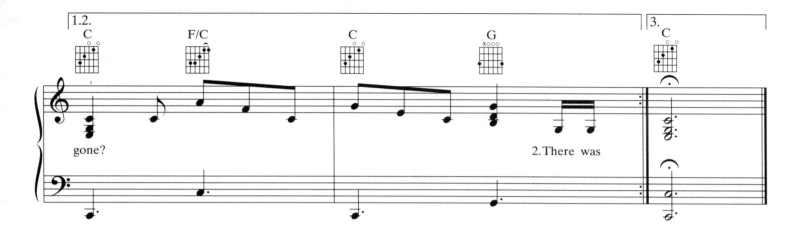

gone?

2. There was

Additional Lyrics

2. There was Bobby and Barry, Paul, Jim and Rick.
   You were so friendly, I was literally sick.
   But when we were alone, I was more or less lost,
   And I'd do what you told me whatever the cost.
   Sometimes I'd come help when you'd babysit kids,
   And for all that we knew, they were dead in their cribs.
   It was late in October, I think, when I heard;
   Everybody was talking and spreading the word,
   Did you hear? Shawn is pregnant. She's keeping the kid,
   And she's not telling anyone who the guy is.
   When I saw you, I didn't know quite what to say,
   Though I wasn't the only one speechless that day.
   A week later, we learned that you'd dropped out of school,
   And all your old suitors were playing it cool.
   So I went to your house, and I climbed up your tree,
   And all that I knew was it couldn't be me...
   But you had left town, and you never came back.
   Later we learned that the baby was black. *(To Chorus)*

3. Now it's twenty years later, and I'm still the guy
   With the fly-away hair and the smoke in his eye.
   It's our high school reunion, and everyone's here,
   Playing down the effects of the drugs and the beer.
   We are balding and gray, overweight, or just tired.
   And so is the rock-and-roll band someone hired.
   Rick and Barry, Paul, Jim and Bob
   Are all happy and healthy, though Jim lost his job.
   We are married with children, and mortgages too,
   And we can't believe all the things we used to do.
   We can still sing along to that song by the Byrds,
   Though it's harder each year to remember the words.
   We can look back and laugh, and the memories are warm;
   We can still raise a glass to the old blue and orange.
   But the music is playing, a song from that year,
   And all I can think is that you should be here.
   Because while we wax nostalgic, or wistful, or sad,
   Still we celebrate something that you never had:
   A chance to grow slowly, a chance to find peace;
   You became an adult in just thirty-six weeks.
   And while we were enjoying the time to be young,
   You were somewhere alone taking care of your son.
   It's not mine to say, to forgive, or forget,
   And I wouldn't presume that you're full of regrets.
   But I wish you could see how we've turned into men,
   Now that we're all reunited again.
   And I wish I could see you, though I can't make amends
   For abandoning you when you needed your friends.
   And I wish I could know that you're doing all right,
   'Cause your name has come up several times tonight.
   It was a magical mystery tour we were on,
   And a long winding road we're still traveling, Shawn...
   When I was fifteen and a man of the world,
   I was madly in love with a Catholic girl.

Entering Marion

Words and Music by
John Forster

Omit 2nd time

way there's a vil-lage called Mar - i - on that you pass through.
driv - ing all morn-ing I came to the top of a hill,

The first time I ap-proached it, I'll al - ways re-mem-ber the
where a sign stood be - fore me that

sign that came in - to view. It said, "En - ter - ing
prom - ised a new kind of thrill. It said, "En - ter - ing

Mar - i - on," and I thought, What a fun lit - tle sign! But the
Bev - er - ly," which was love - ly and not o - ver - built. And the

well. A-round mid-night I pulled in-to Ath-ol____ and

flopped in a flea-bag mo-tel.

I slept

fit-ful-ly in my cloth - ing,

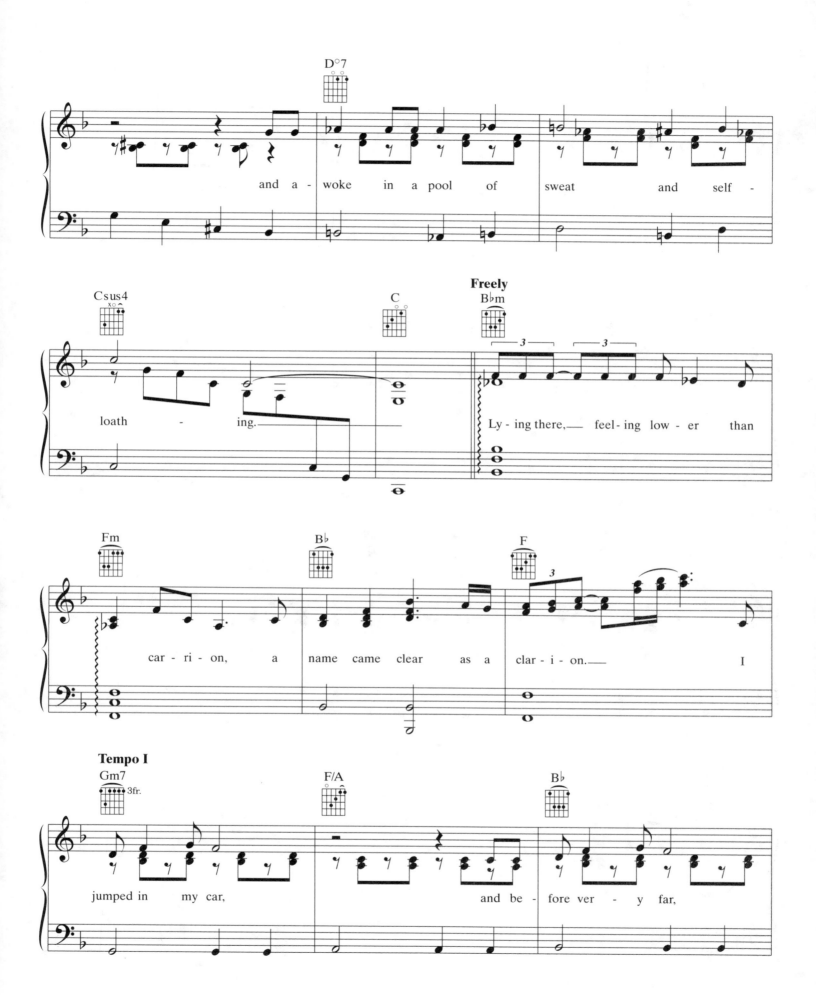

Further And Further Away

Words and Music by
Cheryl Wheeler

1. I can see the place where I came from,
2.3. *See additional lyrics*

I can hear those sounds right now.

*Recorded a half step higher.

I can find the paths____ I used to run

and be-lieve I still____ know____ how.____

Chorus

And then I shake my head,____ clear-ing____ my vi-

sion,____ I keep those scenes____ at____ bay.____

And I can see the place where I
And I can feel the way I used
And I can hear the songs you used

came from
to feel slip-ping fur - ther and fur - ther a-way.
to sing

2. I can

ther and fur - ther a-way,_____ slip-ping

fur - ther and fur - ther a-way._____

Additional Lyrics

2. I can feel the way I used to feel
   When the world was small and green.
   You sang a song of soft appeal
   And I curled into my dreams. *(To Chorus)*

3. I can hear the songs you used to sing,
   I can swear I won't let go.
   You were strong and you knew everything.
   That was all I had to know. *(To Chorus)*

Is It Wrong To Feel So Good
(At This Time In My Life)

Words and Music by
Cliff Eberhardt

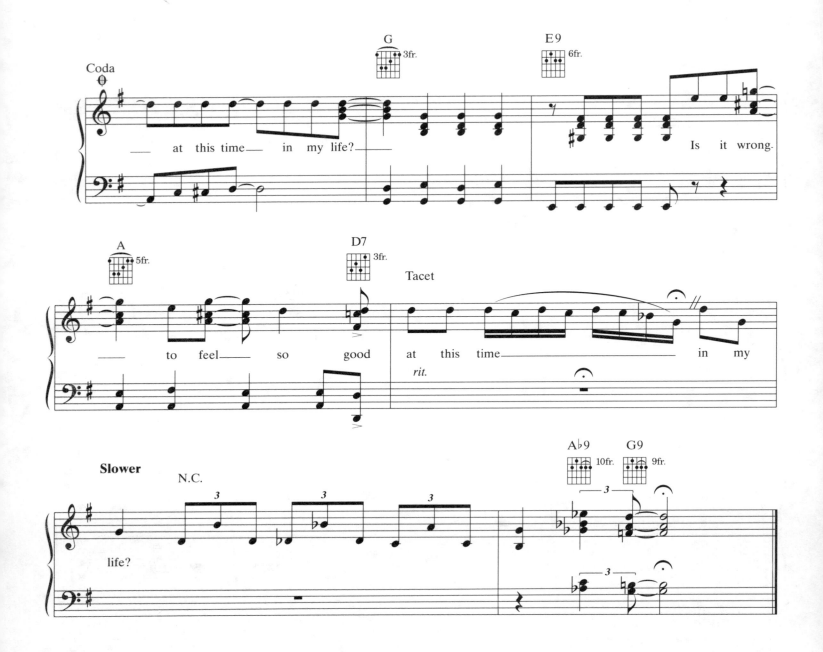

Additional Lyrics

2. I'm all out of money, but my love life is good;
I don't do like I want, I don't do like I should.
Is it wrong to feel so good at this time in my life? *(To Bridge)*

3. I don't win at the races, but I get my share;
I'm unlucky at cards, but I've got someone who cares.
Is it wrong to feel so good at this time in my life? *(To Bridge)*

4. *Repeat 3rd Verse*

Chained To These Lovin' Arms

Words and Music by
Patty Larkin

1. Well, he's lived here all his life,
2.3.4. *See additional lyrics*

him and his farm-er wife, with Je - sus to be-lieve in. And there's

*Guitarists: Tune 6th string down to D. Chord diagrams without names are alternate fingerings of Dsus2.

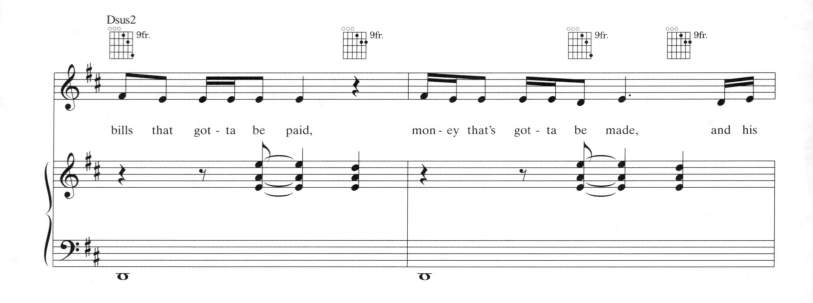

bills that got-ta be paid, mon-ey that's got-ta be made, and his

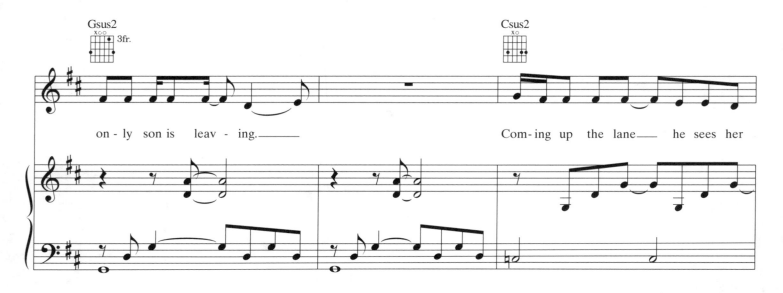

on-ly son is leav - ing._____ Com-ing up the lane____ he sees her

stand-ing there, and he lays____ his head up-on her arms____ and rests it there.__ And he's

Chorus

chained to these lov - in' arms,————— chained——— to these lov - in' arms,

nev - er gon-na leave— them.————— Chained to these lov-in' arms,—————

chained to these lov-in' arms,— and nev-er gon-na leave.

1.

2. They all

Love don't come eas - y, _____ that's a fact. _____ Ain't

ev - er turn - ing back the hands of time, _____ least not yet. _____

Additional Lyrics

2. They all said that her life's a mess,
   They all laughed at her borrowed dress.
   There's nobody gonna teach them.
   She was married at seventeen
   In the cold New Jersey rain
   By a judge, not a preacher.
   They say good things come to those who wait,
   But she'll be damned if she's left standing at heaven's gate.
   And she's... *(To Chorus)*

3. Well, they moved there in the fall
   To the streets of Montreal,
   The singer and the poet.
   But the words never seemed to rhyme
   And the songs sounded out of time,
   Though they tried not to show it.
   Three flights up the stairs in a rented flat,
   They held on to each other tight and they never did look back.
   And they're... *(To Chorus)*

4. If I was a saint I would not cry,
   If I knew better I'd just get by.
   If I was a child I wouldn't worry,
   But all they understand is a poker face
   And a winning hand.
   Go tell it to the jury.
   Well, now, dreams are not the only stuff of life.
   I know that well, 'cause I'm lying safe and sound in your arms tonight.
   And I'm... *(To Chorus)*

Afro-Cuban Lullaby

Words and Music by
Arranged by Jack Marshall and
Christopher Parkening

Tune 6th string down to D

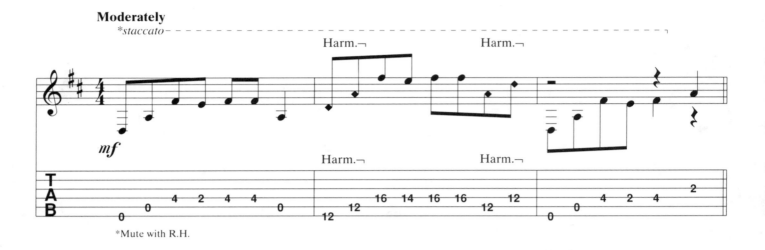

*Mute with R.H.

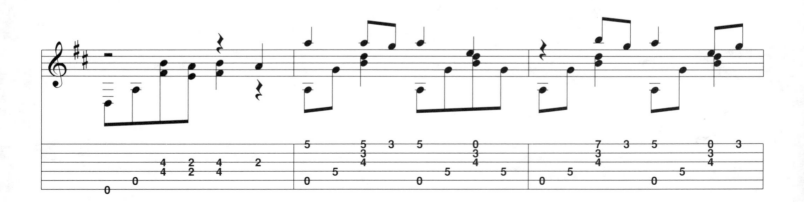

D.S. al Coda

%

staccato

Coda

Harm.⌐   Harm.⌐

rit.

Harm.⌐   Harm.⌐

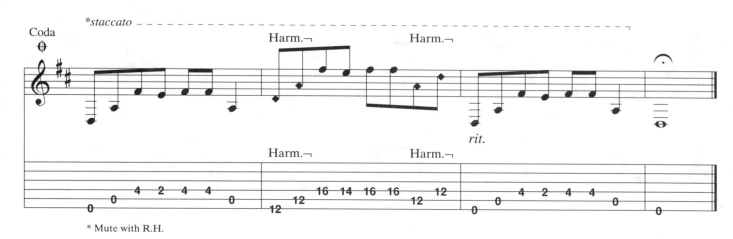

* Mute with R.H.

The Star-Spangled Banner and Me

Words and Music by
David Roth

Moderately fast, freely

A cappella

I was mind-ing my own bus-'ness with a mug of herb-al tea; I

hear the ring-ing of the phone, I an-swer, it's for me. "I'm so-and-so and such-and-such and

I do this and that. I work for the Chi-ca-go Bulls, and I won-der, can we chat. The

coach asked me to call you up, it seems he's heard you sing and won-ders if your tal-ents to Chi-

ca-go we could bring to sing the Na-tional An-them on a na-tion'lly tel-e-vised game. It's

all sold out," he says to me. I says to him, "Who's play-in'?" "The Bulls a-gainst the New York Knicks," he

rap-id-ly re-plied. "I'll have to check my book," I said, and cupped the phone and cried, "My

prayers are an-swered, thank you Lord, I al-ways knew you would." I pick the phone back up a-gain and

say, "I s'pose I could. Just one lit-tle i-tem, though, be-fore we close this deal: A-

mer-i-ca the Beau-ti-ful just might have more ap-peal. Some-thing 'bout those burst-ing bombs, I've

al-ways kind of spurned it." He said, "Star-Span-gled Ban-ner, Mis-ter Roth," and so I learned it. I

show up at the Sta-di-um, the crowd is fill-ing out, eigh-teen thou-sand six hun-dred and

sev-en-ty-six, a-bout. I take my place at cen-ter court, I'm stand-ing on the Bull. I

lift my head to look a-round, the place is freak-ing full. So there I am, I start the song, but

not my u-sual way, not like the whin-y folk-sing-er you're look-ing at to-day. I

raise my voice, I let 'er rip with pas-sion, verve, and style. I go to hit the high-est note, the

place is go-ing wild.   I   fin-ish with a flour-ish "...and the   home   of   the

brave."_____   I   could-'ve sworn I heard the whole crowd chant-ing   "Dave...Dave...Dave..." Tri-

um-phant-ly   I   leave the court, an   ush-er guides my way.   I   guess I'll take my seat there on the

bench with Mi-chael J.   In-stead we take a   cou-ple turns, the   next thing that   I   knew we're

half-way   up   to heav-en   in   the   mez-za-nine, it's true.   I   look a-round, I'm shocked, I'm stunned, it's

hot dogs, pea-nuts, beer,   ox-y-gen, bi-noc-u-lars, that's   all they sell up here.   So

in   a some-what stri-dent voice I   grab my friend and claim,   "I   can't be-lieve they stuck us   way up

here   to watch this game."   Im-me-diate-ly   the wom-an   to   my   right does one of these: "Just

what ex-act-ly's wrong with this lo-ca-tion?" she de-crees.   "We   come to ev-'ry game," she says, "and

this is where we sit. These are our sea-son's tick-ets, sir, and you are full of en-vy." And

then she does a dou-ble take and breath-i-ly mum-bles, "Oh... are you the one who sang the Na-tional

An-them down be-low?" My chest be-gins to swell with pride, I'm rec-og-nized, I guess. With

ev-'ry ounce of wit, pa-nache, and charm I an-swer, "Yes." I'm pull-ing out my pen, she prob-'ly

wants my au-to-graph. In-stead she says, "Gee, u-sually they get fa-mous

peo-ple to do that." There's lit-tle more to re-count in this poig-nant par-a-digm. The

Bulls went on to win that game by one in o-ver-time. And I went on to eat a slice of

hum-ble pie de-light, for you u-sually get what you de-

serve, and I got mine that____ night.

A Folksinger Earns Every Dime

Words and Music by
David Buskin, Abra Bigham
and Robin Batteau

Moderately

A cappella

1. Come all you fine miners and weld-ers of steel,
2.3.4. *See additional lyrics*

come all you farm-ers out stand-ing in fields. I'll

tell you a sto-ry of toil and of strife, and the

hard-ships that come with a folk-sing-er's life. Well, it's

up in the morn-ing as ear-ly as ten,

and it's yes-ter-day's cof-fee, or make some a-gain.

But you got-ta get roll-ing, 'cause it's al-most noon;

the show is at eight, and there's twelve strings to tune. And it's

*Recorded a half step lower.
**3rd time, omit 1st half of Verse.

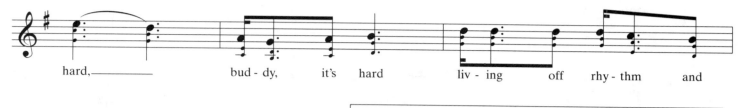

hard,_____ bud - dy, it's hard liv - ing off rhy - thm and

rhyme. And it's hard,_____ Bucko, it's hard. A folk - sing - er earns ev - 'ry

dime. 2. Your Wood - y, it's hard. A folk - sing - er earns ev - 'ry dime.

Additional Lyrics

2. Your fingers are sore from the concert last night,
But you gotta ignore it, there's folksongs to write,
'Bout people 'n' places 'n' hard luck 'n' things;
Wherever there's trouble, a folksinger sings.
Or you're out on the road where the living is hell;
You might even get stuck in some two-star hotel
Where they haven't got Showtime and the bedspread is creased,
And room service takes twenty minutes at least.

2nd Chorus:
And it's hard, fella, it's hard
Living off rhythm and rhyme.
And it's hard, amigo, it's hard;
A folksinger earns every dime.

3. And you're off to the hoot where you're having bad luck;
They yell out, "Sing 'Love Shack' "; they yell out, "You suck!"
And the waitress, she's faithless, she's threatening to quit;
She just looked at your tip and said, "What is this...?"

3rd Chorus:
Sure, and it's hard, hoo boy, it's hard
Living off rhythm and rhyme.
And it's hard, dude, it's hard;
A folksinger earns every dime.

4. You're playing a festival south of the Smokies
On a stool full of splinters in a field full of folkies.
And Paxton is late, so you gotta keep strummin',
When a man cries, "Look out! There's a mime troupe a-comin'!"
Your blood starts to freeze and your skin starts to crawl;
They're doing the "robot," they're doing the "wall."
It's like a bad dream or a weird déjà vu
Of the Great Mime Disaster of '72.

4th Chorus:
And it's hard, Muffy, it's hard
Living off rhythm and rhyme.
And it's hard, Woody, it's hard;
A folksinger earns every dime.

I Am My Dad

Words and Music by
Andrew Ratshin

59

Nod Over Coffee

Words and Music by
Mark Heard

1. All the un-said words that I might be think-ing,_____
2.3.4. *See additional lyrics*

*On D.S., play Verse twice before proceeding to Pre-chorus.

uh_____ huh.

And all the lit-tle signs_____ that

*Guitarists: Use open-E tuning (low to high): E B E G♯ B E.

smile o-ver cof-fee and turn— to go. We know the drill— and we do—

— it well. We love it, we hate it. Ain't that— life.

Chorus

Oh,— ain't that the curse of the sec-ond hand.

1st time, D.S. (take 2nd ending) 𝄋;
2nd time, D.S. (repeat Chorus) al Coda 𝄌

Woh.

Coda

yeah.

Additional Lyrics

2. If I weren't so afraid and alone, uh huh,
   They might pay me what I am worth, uh huh.
   But it would not be enough.
   You deserve better.

   2nd Pre-chorus:
   So we nod over coffee and say goodbye,
   Do whatever has to be done again today.
   Get in that traffic and time will fly.
   Look at the sun and pray for rain.*(To Chorus)*

3. The dam of time, it cannot hold back, uh huh,
   The dust that will surely come of these bones, uh huh.
   And I will not have loved enough,
   Will not have loved enough.

4. If we could see with wiser eyes, uh huh,
   All that is good and is so sad and so true,
   Still it would not be enough,
   Could never be enough.

   3rd Pre-chorus:
   So we nod over coffee and say goodbye,
   Bolt the door, it's time to go.
   Out in the car with the radio on,
   Roll down the window and blow the horn. *(To Chorus)*

A Road Worth Walking Down

Words and Music by
Greg Greenway

*Guitarists: Use open-G tuning (low to high): DGDGBD.

*Pianists: Omit vocal melody next five bars
(next two bars on repeat).

71

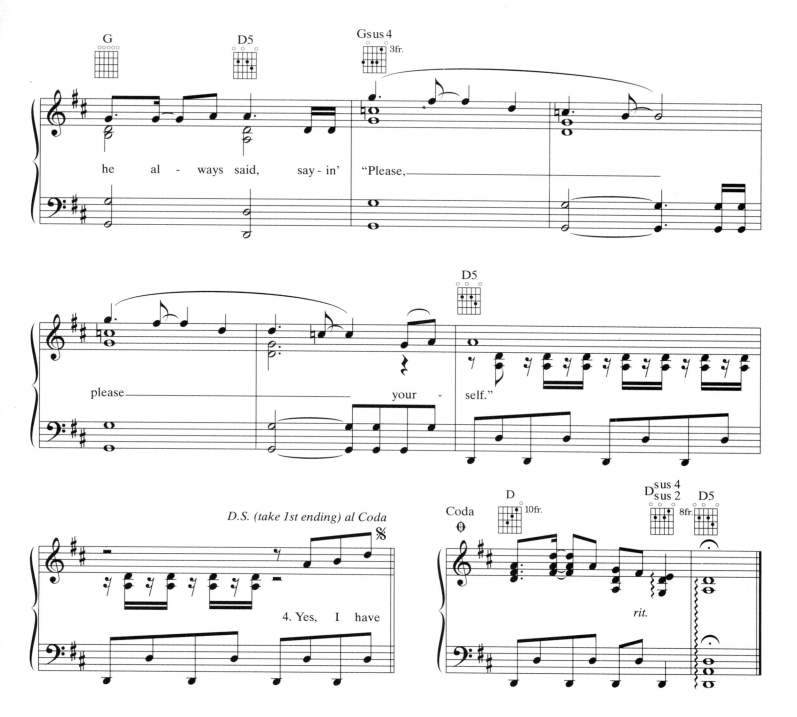

Additional Lyrics

3. Sometimes it rises up inside you,
   Sometimes I feel that I may drown,
   And vanish without ever saying,
   This is my life, this is my ground.
   And I wonder, if my mind is so blinded,
   I won't know it when I've found
   A road worth walking down. (*To Bridge*)

4. Yes, I have seen my mother's courage.
   You gave them life, you let them go.
   And I have chosen my own direction,
   So far away, so far away from it all.
   And I wonder, if my heart is so blinded,
   I won't know it when I've found
   A road worth walking down, *etc.*

Little Piece At A Time

Words and Music by
David Wilcox

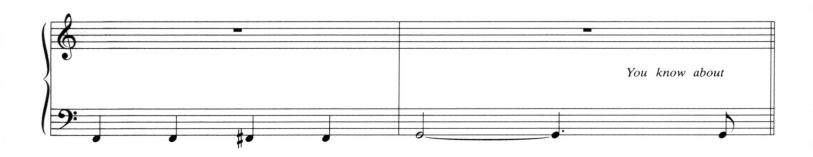

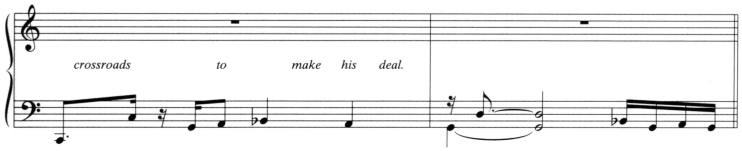

*Guitarists: Use open C tuning (low to high): CGCGCE.

only read the big print,

only read the big print,

only read the big print, the deal looks like it pays.

But

souls are bought just a little bitty piece at a time these days.

A TIME TO DECIDE

Did you ever stand on the ledges
On the brink of a great plateau
And look from her jagged edges
On the country that lay below

When the vision meets no resistance
And there's nothing to stop the gaze
'Til the mountain peaks in the distance
Stand wrapped in a purple haze

There the things that you thought were strongest
And the things that you thought were great
And for which you'd striven for longest
Seemed to carry but little weight

And when you gaze on that vision
And your outlook's so clear and wide
If you have to make a decision
That's the time and place to decide

For should you return to the city
And mingle again with the throng
And your heart gets softened with pity
Or bitter from strife and wrong

Though others may laugh in derision
And the voice of the past grows dim
Remember the cool decision
You made that day on the rim

Bruce Kiskaddon

Endless Sky

Words and Music by
Chuck Pyle

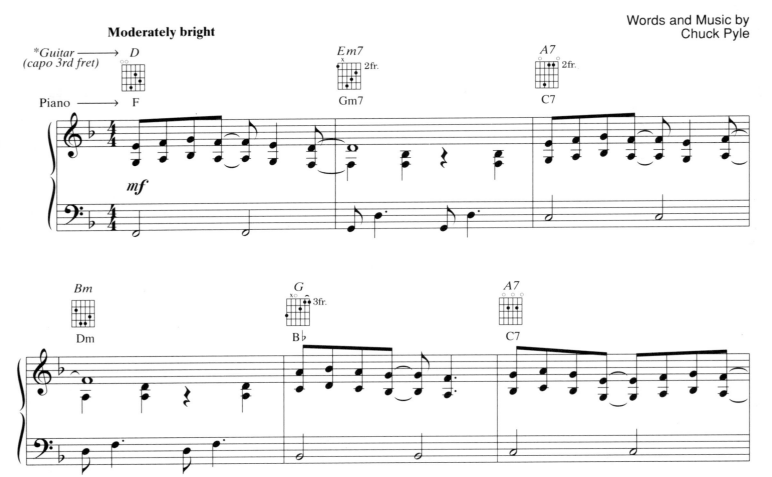

*Guitarists: Tune 6th string down to D, then place capo at 3rd fret.

82

Additional Lyrics

2. I've traded in my working spurs
   For a life of the "His and Hers."
   She's one of a kind, Lord, I know I'm one lucky guy.
   Besides, nothin's quite the same.
   This cowboyin's gettin' too tame.
   And the roof of a pickup takes up too much of the sky. *(To Chorus)*

Shivering

Traditional

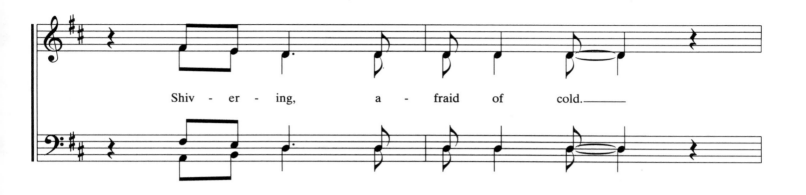

Shiv - er - ing, a - fraid of cold.___

Shiv - er - ing, a - fraid of cold.___

Shiv - er - ing, a - fraid of cold.___

D.C. (with one repeat) al Fine

Yo yo yo yo yo yo.___

The Date
(Making Mountains Out Of Molehills)

Words and Music by
Barbara Kessler

1. If you don't ask me I won't tell you
3. *See additional lyrics*

a-bout the me that came before the one that met you.

Cadd9 / Ebadd9   G / Bb   D/F# / F/A

— sev-en thir-ty, but— you'll prob-a-bly— be late.— And I'll— pre-tend—

Cadd9 / Ebadd9   G / Bb   D/F# / F/A

— I was-n't wait - ing by— the win - dow. And you'll

Cadd9 / Ebadd9   G / Bb   D/F# / F/A

com-ment on the park - ing, and you'll ask a-bout— the pho-tos.— Oh, I had

Chorus

Am / Cm   C/G / Eb/Bb   D/F# / F/A

pie in the sky— dreams.— When you

90

Mak- ing moun - tains out of mole - hills a - gain. Mak - ing moun - tains a - gain.

Additional Lyrics

3. And over dinner you'll tell stories,
   And I will smile and nod politely as always.
   And nothing you say will remind me,
   But there it will be, like footsteps suddenly behind me.

4. Now you might ask, "Is something wrong?"
   Oh, if I let you, you'd find it out before too long.
   It's not that I have regrets.
   I'm just no good at stories that haven't ended yet. *(To Chorus)*

5. And then you'll walk me to the front door.
   It's always just one moment that decides your evermore.
   And if you kiss me, or if you don't,
   I'll wonder what that means and if you'll call or if you won't. *(To Chorus)*

Tight Jeans Round

Words and Music by
Kristina Olsen

With a light swing

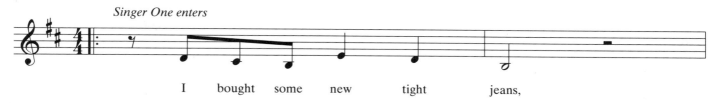

A cappella
Singer One enters

I bought some new tight jeans,

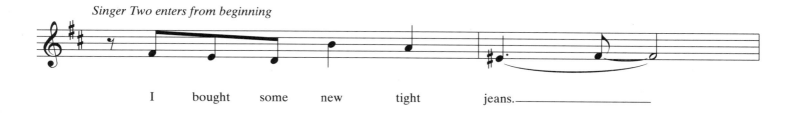

Singer Two enters from beginning

I bought some new tight jeans.___

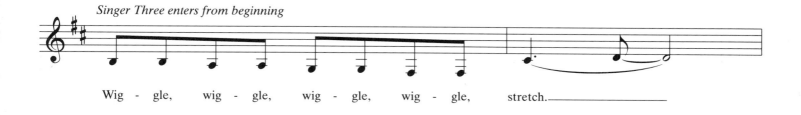

Singer Three enters from beginning

Wig - gle, wig - gle, wig - gle, wig - gle, stretch.___

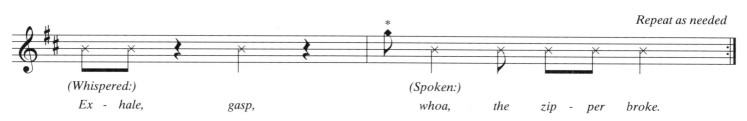

Repeat as needed

(Whispered:)

Ex - hale, gasp,

(Spoken:)

whoa, the zip - per broke.

*Place finger inside of cheek and release to make a popping sound.

Nursery Rhyme Round

Traditional

Moderately

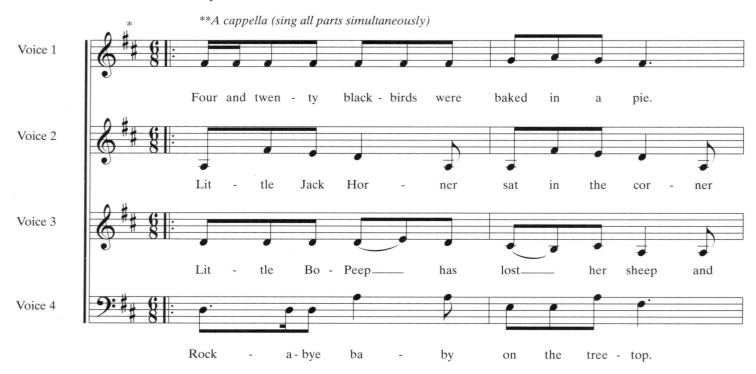

**A cappella (sing all parts simultaneously)

Voice 1: Four and twen - ty black - birds were baked in a pie.

Voice 2: Lit - tle Jack Hor - ner sat in the cor - ner

Voice 3: Lit - tle Bo - Peep has lost her sheep and

Voice 4: Rock - a - bye ba - by on the tree - top.

Four and twen - ty black - birds were baked in a pie.

eat - ing his Christ - mas, Christ - mas pie.

does - n't know where to find them.

When the wind blows the cra - dle will rock.

* Recorded a half step lower.

**Although all four parts are sung simultaneously on the recording, the best way to perform this is as follows:
1st time, Voice 4 sings alone; 2nd time, Voice 1 is added; 3rd time Voice 2 is added; 4th time all sing.

When the pie was o - pen, the bird - ies did sing.

Stuck in his thumb and pulled out a plum,

Leave them a - lone and they will come home,

When the bough breaks the cra - dle will fall, and

Was - n't that a daint - y dish to set be - fore the king?

said, what a good lit - tle boy____ am I!"

wag - ging their tails____ be - hind____ them.

down will come ba - by, cra - dle and all.

Round And Round

Traditional

Moderately bright

A cappella

Singer One enters

Round and round we turn, we hold_____ each oth - er's hands and

Singer Two enters from beginning

weave our - selves in a cir - cle. The

Singer Three enters from beginning   *Repeat as needed*

time is gone, the dance goes on.

BIG TIMES IN A SMALL TOWN

James Mee • *vocal and guitar*

James has lots of wonderful songs like this one—he writes exquisite portraits of rural American life, has recorded two albums, **American Sky** and **Backroad to Mainstreet**, and has just completed a brand new album, **Someday** (Metrostar Records, PO Box 5807, Englewood, NJ 07631). For concert booking and albums-by-mail, write to him at PO Box 1441, Castleton, VT 05735.

Photo: Vincent Nicoletti

DOG DREAMS

Jonatha Brooke • *vocal and guitar*

Patty Larkin • *accordion*
David Buskin • *piano*
David Wilcox, David Roth, Nance Pettit • *harmony vocals*

Jonatha Brooke, besides being a fabulous solo performer, is also one-half of the group The Story (Jennifer Kimball is the other half), which has two albums out, **Grace In Gravity**, and a brand new one, **The Angel In The House**, both on Elektra. For booking information, contact Fleming/Tamulevich & Associates, 733/735 N. Main St., Ann Arbor, MI 48104; phone (313) 995-9066. As of now, Jonatha's dogs are still on the Massachusetts "Most Wanted" list.

Photo: Roger Gordy

IS IT WRONG TO FEEL SO GOOD
(AT THIS TIME IN MY LIFE)

Cliff Eberhardt • *vocal and guitar*

Originally from Paoli, PA, now living in New York City, Cliff Eberhardt is one of the best songwriters around. He's got one album out so far, **The Long Road**, on Windham Hill. He performed solo at the retreat, but he's also incredibly great with a band. Go see him. Trust me. For concert booking, contact Katherine Moran & Associates, PO Box 60, Weare, NH 03281; phone (603) 529-1545; fax (603) 529-7545.

Photo: Cathy Cox

ENTERING MARION

John Forster • *vocal and piano*

I first heard John Forster on WXRK in New York when Vin Scelsa played John's demo cassette on his Sunday night radio program, *"Idiot's Delight."* After getting over my instant jealousy (what a writer! what a mind!), I contacted Vin, got a copy of that demo, and was blown apart by the most insightful, clever writing I'd heard in *years*. The big news is that John Forster's debut album has just been completed, conveniently titled **Entering Marion**. It is issued by Rounder/Philo, and is available by mail from Limousine Records, PO Box 196, Nyack, NY 10960. It's sensational. For booking information, contact Moran & Associates (see Cliff's, above).

Photo: Carol Rosegg, Martha Swope Associates

NOD OVER COFFEE

Pierce Pettis • *vocal and guitar*

Geoff Bartley • *guitar*
Nancy Moran, Hugh Blumenfeld • *harmony vocals*

Born and raised in Fort Payne, Alabama, now living in Atlanta, Pierce Pettis dropped in and out of the retreat a couple of times—he put together this group in the afternoon, sang it that night for the first time—Hugh, Nancy, and Geoff did a terrific job. Pierce writes most of his own music (he's a *genius*), but he also does great covers—this song was written by the late Mark Heard, producer of Pierce's album **Tinseltown**. (A new compilation of Mark's work, entitled **High Noon**, can be obtained by writing to Fingerprint Music, PO Box 197, Merrimac, MA 01860.) To book Pierce Pettis, contact Ray Ware Artist Management, (615) 790-7820. His three albums to date: **Chase The Buffalo**, **Tinseltown** (Windham Hill/High Street), and **While The Serpent Lies Sleeping** (Windham Hill). He also appears on the compilations **Legacy** and **Winter Solstice III**. Windham Hill, PO Box 9388, Stanford, CA 94309; phone (415) 329-0647.

Photo: Gil Williams

FURTHER AND FURTHER AWAY

Cheryl Wheeler • *guitar and vocal*

This is the most unusual live recording of Cheryl Wheeler you are ever going to find—mostly because you hear her just singing here, not talking. At her live concerts she sometimes goes off on the most hilarious impromptu monologues, almost forgetting she's a singer and songwriter—but this song is a reminder of just how truly great she is. Her albums to date are: **Cheryl Wheeler** and **Half A Book** on North Star Records; **Circles And Arrows** on Philo/Rounder; and her brand new **Driving Home** on Philo/Rounder. For bookings, contact Concerted Efforts, PO Box 99, Newtonville, MA 02160.

Photo: Beverly Parker

SUMMER OF LOVE

Peter Nelson • *keyboard and vocal*

Peter makes his living as a journalist, contributing regularly to magazines such as *Esquire*, but he is also a novelist, and as you can hear, he's a superb songwriter, too. I first heard about him through the ravings of John Gorka, then David Wilcox performed Peter's song "Old" in concert (knocked me out). This song is just a sample of his work—I hope he'll do an entire album someday soon. For booking information, contact him at 160 Main St., Northampton, MA 01060; phone/fax (413) 586-2215.
P.S. Peter's wife, Diane, was named the retreat's official "Gravy Queen."

Photo: Paul Shoul

AFRO-CUBAN LULLABY

Hilary Field • *guitar*

It was a real treat to have a guitarist like Hilary Field in our midst. One night at The Wintertide Coffeehouse we celebrated the release of her debut album, **Music Of Spain & Latin America** on Yellow Tail Classics; later that week a group of us sat with Hilary around the dining room table at the Sea Spray Inn and listened to radio station WMVY play it (it was the first time Hilary *ever* heard herself on the radio); and *then*, while working on the liner notes for *this* album, we get word that **Music Of Spain & Latin America** has been nominated as "Classical Album Of The Year" by the National Association of Independent Record Distributors! Hilary's having a great year. For concert, booking, and fan club information—it's the same as **Electric Bonsai Band's** (below).

Photo: Karen Moscowitz

THE STAR-SPANGLED BANNER AND ME

David Roth • *vocal*

For everyone who's ever wondered what it's like to sing The National Anthem at a sporting event, well, now you know. David is one multi-faceted, multi-talented man, also a great guitarist and pianist. His albums to date are: *Rising In Love, I'll Be Here For You, Another Side of David Roth*, and *Nights At The Chez*, available through PO Box 1174, Old Chelsea Station, New York, NY 10011-0910. For concert booking contact Real Arts Productions, 145 Mountain Rd., Rosendale, NY 12472, phone (914) 658-3467.

Photo: Carole Levingston

A FOLKSINGER EARNS EVERY DIME

David Buskin • *lead vocal, lead clapper*

Jonatha Brooke, Kristina Olsen, David Roth, Christine Lavin, Sally Fingerett, Greg Greenway *harmony vocals, harmony clappers*

This song not only blows the lid off the world of glam-folk, it's an example of a singer losing complete control of a song in mid-performance, then snatching it back in an instant. Besides being a world-class singer *and* clapper, David Buskin is an ace guitarist and pianist as well. His albums include *He Used To Treat Her* (Epic; out of print); two *Pierce Arrow* albums on Columbia (out of print); four *Buskin & Batteau* albums (some stock remaining—write to PO Box 793, Village Station, NY, NY 10014); and he also sang tasteful harmonies on Judy Collins' beautiful album *Fires Of Eden*. David has just completed a brand new solo album, *Heaven Is Free Tonight* (write to address above). For concert booking, call (212) 662-9693.

Photo: Joe Henson

I AM MY DAD

Electric Bonsai Band • *vocal and guitar*

Yes, I know, it's not electric and it's not a band, but if you know Andrew Ratshin, you know he doesn't do things like anyone else. After years as the guiding force behind the trio *Uncle Bonsai, Electric Bonsai Band* is his newest brilliant creation, and under this name he has recorded three albums, *I Am Joe's Eyes, 20 Seconds of Pleasure*, and *But I'm Happy Now*, which includes a studio version of *I Am My Dad*. (Andrew also has *another* band in Seattle called *Mel Cooleys*. He is one hard-working guy.) For mail order information, write to Yellow Tail Records, 9102 17th Avenue NE, Seattle, WA 98115-3212. For concert booking write to that address to the attention of Ebb Productions. Phone numbers for both are (206) 525-3546. For fan club information, the address is the same; the phone number is different: (206) 527-3546.

Photo: John Anderson

CHAINED TO THESE LOVIN' ARMS

Patty Larkin • *vocal and guitar*

You already know Patty plays a mean acoustic accordion, but here she shows off what really sets her apart—her fabulous voice and guitar playing. But that's not all she can do—at the retreat one morning she even cooked pancakes for everyone (yes, *Pattycakes!*). Her concert schedule takes her all over the map, and she's recorded four albums: *Tango* on High Street/Windham Hill, *Live In The Square, I'm Fine* and *Step Into The Light* on Philo/Rounder. She is currently working on a new High Street album to be released later this year. For concert booking information contact Fleming/Tamulevich & Associates, 733/735 N. Main, St., Ann Arbor, MI 48104; phone (313) 995-9066.

Photo: John F. Cooper

A ROAD WORTH WALKING DOWN

Greg Greenway • *vocal and guitar*

Greg is one of the best new singer/songwriters to emerge from the Boston music scene and was a favorite with audiences *and* basketball players at the retreat. He has recorded one album, ***A Road Worth Walking Down,*** which is available through the mail by writing to Face Productions, PO Box 426, Astor Station, Boston, MA 02123-0426. For booking information, contact Robert Haigh, Lands End Promotions, 11 Poplar Lane, N. Chelmsford, MA 01863; phone (617) 224-0300 or (508) 251-3546.

Photo: Susan Wilson

THE DATE
(MAKING MOUNTAINS OUT OF MOLEHILLS)

Barbara Kessler • *vocal and guitar*

Barbara is another great new voice coming out of the Boston scene—she came by one night, we were only able to make room for her to sing this one song—and she just nailed it in performance, so here it is. Right now she has one cassette available, ***Barbara Kessler Live***—for that and for concert booking, contact Johnny Brock Management, 51 Maxfield St., W. Roxbury, MA 02132; phone (617) 327-6470.

Photo: Craig Harris

LITTLE PIECE AT A TIME

David Wilcox • *vocal and guitar*

From Asheville, North Carolina, David burst upon the national music scene a few short years ago and has quickly become one of the most popular performers working today. He has recorded three albums: ***Home (Again) For the First Time*** and ***How Did You Find Me Here*** on A&M, and ***Nightshift Watchman*** on Black Mountain Music (he's working on a brand new A&M album that will be released later this year). For concert booking, contact Terry Rindel at (818) 995-2475; for fan club information write to Russel Carter Management, 315 W. Ponce de Leon, Suite 755, Decatur, GA 30030; phone (404) 377-9900.

Photo: Alison Shaw

A TIME TO DECIDE/ENDLESS SKY

Chuck Pyle • *vocal and guitar*

The poem that opens this piece was written by Bruce Kiskaddon from a book called ***Rhymes Of The Ranges*** (Hollywood: Earl Hayes, 1924)—and Chuck wants you to know that this was the first time he recited it, and he got a couple of the words wrong (to get the *exact* lines, see p.80). Chuck lives and performs mostly out west—we got this recording when he stopped by the open mike one Thursday night at The Wintertide. Albums to date include ***Endless Sky, Step By Step***, and ***Drifter's Wind.*** For concert booking, mail order and correspondence, write to Chuck at Bee'n'Flower Music, Box 385, Eldorado Springs, CO 80025; phone (303) 494-7225.

Photo: Courtesy Chuck Pyle

:::: T
:::: H
:::: E
::::
:::: A
:::: R
:::: T
:::: I
:::: S
:::: T
:::: S
::::

SHIVERING/TIGHT JEANS ROUND/ NURSERY RHYME ROUND

The Impromptu A Cappella Choir

David Roth, Nancy Moran, Andrew Ratshin, Sally Fingerett, Christine Lavin, Kristina Olsen, David Buskin, Barbara Kessler, David Wilcox, Greg Greenway, Dan Green, Jonatha Brooke, James Mee

David Roth taught us the "Shivering" song (he learned it from a workshop tape by Nick Page, who on the tape says he learned the song from the Zulu tradition), Kristina Olsen led us in her "Tight Jeans Round," and Cheryl Wheeler (not present when we performed it) taught us the "Nursery Rhymes" song. That weird last harmony chord was instigated by Jonatha Brooke. She just goes mental for those 9ths and 13ths. Kristina Olsen has three albums out: *Kristina Olsen* on Philo/Rounder; *Cupid Is Stupid* and *It Don't Take Too Much,* on the Take A Break label (she is currently working on a new album). For concert booking, contact Katherine Moran & Associates (same as Cliff Eberhardt). For correspodence and mail order, write to Take A Break Productions, PO Box 21, Venice, CA 90294-0021. Though you can't hear it here, Kristina also plays acoustic guitar, steel guitar, piano, concertina, hammer dulcimer, and saxophone, and she's a wildly graceful tango dancer. She gave us all lessons one night. Who says musicians can't dance?

Photo: Ek Waller

ROUND AND ROUND

Traditional

David Roth, Nancy Moran, Andrew Ratshin, Sally Fingerett, Christine Lavin, Kristina Olsen, David Buskin, Barbara Kessler, Grant King, David Wilcox, Greg Greenway, Dan Green, Jonatha Brooke, Kate Taylor, James Mee

Tony Lombardi, general manager of The Wintertide Coffeehouse, is the voice you hear making closing remarks.

David Roth taught us this song, too. On all these a cappella songs you can hear a beautiful new voice ringing through—that's Nancy Moran, formerly of Baltimore, now living in Nashville. Keep your eye on her. You can also hear Grant King (who did the graphic design of this artwork), Kate Taylor, who lives on the Vineyard and came by to lend her support, and also Sally Fingerett, my pal in the Bitchin' Babes group and an all-around swell person (she is also the hysterical laugher on the "Star Spangled Banner" song), and the legendary musician/fisherman Dan Green, from Columbus, Ohio. Dan caught a great big giant striped sea bass and fed us all one night. Bruce Schaffner stuffed it with mushrooms. It was delicious and so gosh darn big that the picture of it wouldn't fit into this little book.

Big Times In A Small Town *is available on Philo (PH1155, CD & Cassette)*
Distributed by Rounder Records (call 1•800•44•DISCS}

EXECUTIVE PRODUCER: CHRISTINE LAVIN
PRODUCER/ENGINEER: DAVID SEITZ
COORDINATING PRODUCER: KATHERINE MORAN
GENERAL MANAGER OF THE WINTERTIDE COFFEEHOUSE: TONY LOMBARDI
TECHNICAL DIRECTOR: MARK FRINK
TECHNICAL CONSULTANTS: LLOYD DONNELLY AND FRANK COAKLEY
MIXING: DAVID SEITZ AT THE OPERATING ROOM, GREAT NECK, NY
EDITING AND ASSEMBLY: MARK AVNET AT THE MAGIC SHOP, NYC
SPIRITUAL ADVISOR: STEVE ROSENTHAL
PUBLICITY MANAGER: CANDY GIANETTI
STAGE MANAGER: KEITH DeSUTTER
ASSISTANT STAGE MANAGER: KEN LINCOLN
TROUBLESHOOTERS: PEGGY TILESTON, SUSANNA STURGIS, BARBARA DACEY
CATERERS: BARBARA VASATURO AND JEAN THORNE
HOUSE MOTHER: RAYEANNE KING AT THE SEA SPRAY
HOUSE FATHER: BRADY AT BRADYS
COVER ARTIST: LIZA COOGAN
COVER TYPOGRAPHY: GRANT KING
ART DIRECTOR: NANCY GIVEN

James Mee appears courtesy of Metrostar Records
Jonatha Brooke appears courtesy of Elektra Records
Pierce Pettis and Patty Larkin appear courtesy of High Street/Windham Hill Records
Sally Fingerett appears courtesy of Amerisound Records
Electric Bonsai Band and Hilary Field appear courtesy of Yellow Tail Records
David Wilcox appears courtesy of A&M Records

Special thanks to Beckie, Alice, Russell, Meghen, Kaf, and the many other volunteers who make the Wintertide happen; to Gregory Bochow for the absolutely best clambake in the world (best because he served us lobsters instead of clams); to that dynamic duet of the music world, guitar instructor Howard Morgen and vocal coach Estelle Morgen, for helping us continue to learn; to yoga instructor Elizabeth Bunker for helping us relax; to Barbara Vasaturo for feeding us fabulous food; to David Seitz, for all the hard work; to Bill Kollar for the post production technical help. . .

. . .and to the owners of these Martha's Vineyard businesses who housed us, spread the word, printed posters, made us feel welcome, and came to our concerts:

The Sea Spray Inn,
2 Nashawena Park, Oak Bluffs

Bradys Bed & Breakfast,
10 Canonicus Avenue, Oak Bluffs

The Narragansett House,
62 Narragansett Street, Oak Bluffs

The Martha's Vineyard Times
The Vineyard Gazette

Tisbury Printer
Marianne's Screen Printing
Vineyard Bottled Waters
Ken Bailey Distributing
Hear-Say CDs and Tapes
Slight Indulgence
The Black Dog Restaurant and Bakery
and WMVY, 92.7 FM, one of the great
radio stations in this country.

We'd also like to thank Peter Primont of Cherry Lane Music, Kevin Sheehan of the HEAR Music Catalog, Pam Lewis of Lewis/Doyle Management, and sound engineers Lloyd Donnelly, Mark Frink, and Frank Coakley, for conducting music business-related workshops during the retreat. And special thanks to Rounder Records for releasing this album.

The Wintertide Coffeehouse, located at Five Corners in Vineyard Haven (1/2 a block from the ferry), is an all-volunteer, non-profit community project, open all year. The mailing address is P.O. Box 29, Vineyard Haven, MA 02568; fone/fax (508) 693-1767; hotline is (508) 693-8830.

Christine Lavin

has recorded six solo albums for Rounder/Philo Records (and is currently working on her seventh). She has produced other compilation albums that you might want to listen to, if you like this one:

When October Goes (Rounder/Philo PH 1143)

On A Winter's Night (North Star 0028)

Buy Me Bring Me Take Me: Don't Mess My Hair!!!
Life According To Four Bitchin' Babes
(Volumes I and II)
(Rounder/Philo PH 1140 and 1150)

For mail-order information write to:
M. Lavin, 313 Mulberry Street, Rochester, NY 14620.

• •

*Look for the matching songbook to Vol. II of **Buy Me Bring Me Take Me: Don't Mess My Hair!!!**, published by Cherry Lane Music (CL02502111), as well as **The Christine Lavin Songbook** (CL02502095), available at your local music dealer or write directly to:*

HLE Hal Leonard Publishing Corporation
7777 West Bluemound Road P.O. Box 13819 Milwaukee, WI 53213

To obtain a limited edition poster of the cover artwork, signed and numbered by Liza Coogan, contact Black Dog Catalog *(508) 693-1991.*

For a free copy of the *Record Roundup* catalogue, call *(800) 44-DISCS.*
For a free copy of the *HEAR* Music Catalog, call *(800) 959-HEAR.*

• •

To obtain information about next year's retreat and a touring concert of
"The Martha's Vineyard Singer/Songwriters' Retreat" contact

Katherine Moran & Associates,
PO Box 60, Weare, NH 03281;
phone (603) 529-1545 / fax (603) 529-7545.

BIG TIMES IN A SMALL TOWN

Thank you all who participated, and to those of you who attended our concerts, and those of you who are listening to this album now—thank you for supporting live music, The Wintertide Coffeehouse, and being part of the spirit that's created when people come together to make music.

—Christine Lavin

Everyone at Cherry Lane Music wishes to express their thanks to Christine Lavin for organizing the First Annual Martha's Vineyard Singer/Songwriters' Retreat. I especially know how much time and energy Chris put into making it a success.

During the short week I spent at the Vineyard, I met so many talented people that at times I thought my head might explode. With the energy that came from all those who participated, I came back to the office knowing our company would find ways to support this worthwhile endeavor.

Since Cherry Lane started publishing folk music in the 60s, we have known that the song is the driving force behind the music industry. Now, in the 90s, the world is awakening to this fact.

I hope that by publishing this songbook, we will encourage writers all over the world to pick up their guitars, learn some new songs, and continue to write.

With best regards to all the writers I know, and those whom I may never meet,

—Peter Primont

THE VINEYARD TAPES